MICRO ASIAN

THE CARROT MAAS BUSINESS

KARANVIR SINGH

ISBN 979-888546063-7

A simple maths after you are done with physics is calculus. Here this book goes into silent invocatins by far the most intelligent feature and a craft par excellence. I dedicate this book to the several teams working accross Carrot InteLLIO Base , Citibank, HDFC, Yes Bank, PNB and ECB & World Bank, Linked In, Instagram & Meta, Wordpress.....

The list moves to the spectacular media services incuding Radio and TV and Internet for the vivid challenge of promotions and venture health.

Long hours of work put into the making this book are a timline apart and the process was enjoyed thoroughly.

Special Thanks;

Dilip Soman, Professor at the Rotman School of Management, University of Toronto. Dilip does research on interesting human behaviours and their applications to consumer welfare, policy and financial literacy. He is also interested in research on poverty, global health, education and development in the global south.

His lectures promoted a feeling of honest entrepreneurship and taught the basic goals of business run on Choice Architecture & BE-Courtesy -Edx.org

Special Thanks:

Ashwani Bakshi, A humble and hands-on award winning leader having international work experience in varying assignments. Proven experience leading sustainable market growth, business planning, and strategy. High-integrity, energetic leader known for delivering proven results and creating successful outcomes that drive organizations forward.Diverse industry and functional expertise, with a tenacious commitment to driving solutions, innovation, and high-quality growth to meet organizational goals with customer delight attitude. He can be contacted on Linked In.

Special Thanks:

Richa Dhodi , A dedicated & hardworking professional with rich experience of 12 years in Media & Entertainment,Pharma, E-Commerce Industries in Content creation, Sales & Marketing, and Operations areas.

She is currently placed with KOO India and Pursuing Executive MBA program from IIM, Kashipur. AN aspiring author.

Lorose

Contents

Foreword

The subject of choice and a material conquest about the world in totality is ethereal and permanent. I saw Micro ASIAN as the front runner of BE in Action and a new inventory of New Age Tools and Puzzles.

Micro ASIAN is the born from antiquity children that i suppose will gather our attention spans and motivate us to deliver our carnage.

Preface

Ever thought how Money is Created and Deployed?? Ever thought how rich is a Central Bank or a Large Cap Funding Body.....

Carrot MaaS was our answer to a sectional authority that gave us new systematic tools to enable the active participation of assets, values and ledgers on our account.

The CHEQUE is Ready!

Checkmate !!

Acknowledgements

Electronic Idea|eFed/eBlue / Revealed Discovery

Mind Or Human Brain is as Complex as the Grains in the Biosphere. Ever Since Computers a Free Knowledge Setup had evolved to look into the possibility of working with them as Technical Affiliates and Specialist. I look back at just the Recent History the year 2013 when I got some real success finding myself being able to create Thoughts and Turn them into Self Transmitted Data Info/Signal going directly into the coverage space a few Feet, Millimetres, or Inside the Brain while shutting off the Eye Lids. It's a practical dream and a miracle that remained incomplete without asking everyone how would they react to such a thing. Generally speaking the Idea became apparent for putting the invention to test , experiment and application in the Wireless Domain to Run, Administer or Control Business Development Freely and Sustainably.

What looks like a Network Inside my mind and body is A Nano Radio*. It's a Robotic Experience and I am excited to see everyone putting a white label to the Greatest Realization on Planet.

Whatever goes behind my startups [BlueFedFin Ixc, Kapple Kape SXCi and CarrotBay SXCi......& others] is the thinking and planning out of the insatiable invention.

To reach every human pocket whether you are a family or individual I believe freedom to choose nature as your greatest ally is the proposed plan to accept the New Normal and Articulate all artistic desire to Design, Create and Innovate the New Universe , A place where Abundance and Caregiving are not just your goals but the specific areas of expertise and interest to occupy every human price Value.

I have been a Poet, A Star Lover, A Multimedia Practitioner, Collaborator, An Insipid Audio Engineer, Author and Entrepreneur but my Common Multiplication went through the Tribunal of Tribulations for not getting back the Potential Care from the Political Bearers. That's where Faith is utterly Important because not only a low Bank Balance but a Low Morality creates ridiculous Pain that doesn't go away easily. That's why I have a dream, A Dream to Capture, Concieve and Collate the World into a Mindful Company that will never run into losses..Sun Kissed...!!

Tapping into your Phone or Desktop on a Friday is often followed by extinguished Memories...RAM Speed and CPU Usage... Follow The Keyboard there is C For Coffee and G For Grace. I hope you get to answer Both .

*Also some of the Details of How and Where it started is Recorded in my Book "The Last Light of God" . Check Your Amazon App and Fetch a Copy.
Love You Insignia.

Prologue

Carrot Server ISE AE⅘ Services -5690900 : 600000 INR XCLi UNiLaw EsQ700

Lorose

Template Chip Cellular and Transactions Between Company-Market-Banks/ 3 Tier Quality Corporation..

Simulation Podcasting On Broadband VoiP For Defence System and Ultra Financial Intelligent Decision Making Process.

Sovereign Debt Resolve- XeroN Indexing.

@Job Code- RRMM50090054700/DE

DOI, CSAT Satellite GSE 11K* 99780p , (-5678-8897-9889-6654-3244)/0010*

Lets follow the fighter jets.....

CHAPTER ONE

A Lions Pocketbook 1.0

Patch, Path, Peacock are not known for a fury against the lion...the sleeping giant theory and the business point of taking the tower to the perfect Pearl.

The patient must visit the pattern or if that is vulnerable is neglected.

MICRO ASIA is the new kingdom of Pocket Economy from space to server a native line of command. The PLAY PLEASE came formally from a casual phone call , while PoWT was a plastic plate on the Globe from a platform by the Hybrid Technology and the wonders of Computing and Cardinal Geometry of the Business in question.

The perfect question is who would sign the plastic affair and be a part of a third world by no means is that a selling station price nor its gonna sell your goods to the plot.

The gigantic victory of the world we have assumed by narratives and stories is now a Micro World.

The Lion's Play is around the dove..

The Settler of the Lord, heavens above.

Lorose

The entire gamut of permutations and combinations tells us the land is blessed by the poem from the skies to the underneath. We cannot disown the craft , our melody and our vivacious culture cannot live on bias , begotten disgust and insults.

I think its format station condition.

I am inclusive, exclusive and C-Suite Market.

That's in the correlation.

A business strategy that will work out on the Micro System is very very complicated in function..We can dissolve the entire dis-functional array and reload the world with a premium paid function and a better life.

My vision here was partially inclined to a traverse path b virtue of which I could reduce the summation of buying genuine stock came to picture.

As Strategy flows down the part of defence there are more neutral grounds to fix business line and format the

K-Universe. Its an equation which normally means your behavior every moment. I have seen that for a long period of time. The elective partition of Asia is normally an anti histamine and an insecure proposition.

> *Peace to the air to the water and the skies be clear.*
> *- Tao Affirmation*

Lorose

Very hard, very impromptu and very humble, Micro Asia is the Central Pool Idea to engrave the future with is its Golden EDGE.

Let me start with Economic Dressing....

You're welcome to the official protocol from PoWT..

Love from Seattle Radio Base & Team FinBlue IN-US.

CHAPTER TWO

Micro ASIA -Who rules the federation?

By all means my sovereignty is formidable. In a free country , free constitution and free selective behaviour I think its very reasonable to unclock the route to reset new windows of supervision and severity. The Democratic Federal Contour will assess this by the next decade and fly pass the next generation its rigid dues.

Humanity...

> *GoldFISH SIX (6) is the cloud that is revered for the smashing hit jungle mix to awaken the tremolo and raise new age banks remove lending and promise each one the right to wealth.*

Lorose

While Project GOLDFISH SIX (6) is air-broadcast and snap cast an obvious choice was to render seprately the security mix to the Governments and the remarkable street fight by PoWT in 2020. Pandemic (COVID 19) was a lateral stage uproar and I was able to compress the time machine into the CEO Office as we were running into Springs and Seasons.

The real expectation of the Funding & Advances was choked in the pipe.

I recall business exchange with Citibank Inc., they were very well received and we had our dues assigned.

2020 was also us giving away more transmission than previous cycle.

The future from the very base station looked greasy.

And before our hands slip I made the traction to result for us The Micro Asia from a Micro asian...

> *Its a free paradise and a free transit system that came to my common sense as the additional WHY.....?*

Lorose

I was getting well on ground and feeling perfect health in the midst of the war making cries coming from the suffering humanity. This is real.. we all make entry on the dice and we all make words bigger and brighter...I was dealing with the cosmic matter.

Micro Asia is a dream and a corner beauty for many.

Let us see our pocket welders case...

CHAPTER THREE

How Airports Can Change Travel Behaviour

Micro Asia is intelligence - Social, Behavioral and Economical. I am thinking about removing the Cash...I am also asking for Free DEBIT & CREDIT Cards. What is the question or the price tag is the Digital Ports.

I think AI has given immense support to the human intelligence abilities and has carved a new age digital economy and Micro Asia is the quintessential frame work of Digitally Connecting the World.

I am a huge fan of air travel and I believe dropping the unpopular base with Airports will exercise complete growth patterns and a unanimous business talk can be acquired and used to asset matching and royalty.

Horizontal Economy:

The beacon of privilege be given to each and every one . Not the poor ....Nor the rich...its the small simple step to Tao and making its grass more dew and more dues. I was fascinated with business finance early in my career. There

I learnt record books and my parental care was divided between reading and writing the finance code.

The HE is the symbolic & sustainable e-route for an equitable equal liquid economy powered by Digital Connectivity.

The Next You will read is the blog entries from the year 2016 and followed...

I consider this to be a very strategic end point connection to my world and the augmented supernatural business class filmsy...

CHAPTER FOUR

Micro ASIA - Stem 1, System 401K

Team -Carrot Intelligence CyBer Sqaure Canada (Server LAX 1.0.13136)

- *Ethernet Sub Cost to Cover Global Economic News & Headlines.-*

ATQ223390. Ethernet 2 EtherNET -Voice Mail Service Via BFF secondory Node

Neural Network. -ATQ 334E66(Law)

- *Gear Shifting between Consumption and Supply SHEDER Gap.-ATQ*

33342W779001Q

- *Application, KPI, Linux Match Service to Bluetooth Printing.- SEATQ*

Service BEN ID Carrot House 11Q -ATQ221000090P (Law) (III)

• *Compact GPS ULE – eNCR-data.gov.cc.iuk.us.eu3.com*

//?112.2.3.1ITPR -ATQ 779000G776 (.Gov)

Team -Carrot Intelligence CyBer Sqaure Canada

Voice Matrix Control Protocol

DI Chip Design 9.0

KloUen One IOspherE 7000K*

IP Cloud Platform

FM Radio PaaS 5050 GSE4.0 Server

–CTO, Project GoldFish SIX(6)2021-2022©

Click VERticON SAT 500 CEO2 TQ Listof Asset Broadband CCS 5000GBPS DebitONInsipian Credit ,XGD,gDPS, GGS

Click SORT Radio Code 1145hZx.c.n.n.t8687890EEE3

Carrot Bay , UK, US, EU , Bold Band Gross Deposit Servïcē.

CARROT BAY 5G IOXC 33.00.00.96

Technology AA 600 Billion $ FinaXCe Development Funds 7865 Million $ Total Recovery RQ 2 AC , 6300 Billion £

Call-Rate Computational , Services , PaperBlueEXO DEddition , IV6800, GA 9000 Trillion €°€°••=•|€|Δ6.0979YBB 2 KKLE 8IOQ

Chip-In-Biological Mass Unit XXAQ 5000 to YESDC 60000000 INR 2 INR Xobe Onē CASE RTP, Bluetooth A.1.1.900 Chip CrotIAN U6, Carrot Bay, Made in India SettingsQ56.78.900.90009.7 Law ,(u) 994E,XSA5,YUR67,XSF77 AUTHENTICID :: PPP9968046E566*

F75D237F91170I669LLFED

Yes Bank , XS 1669 to 1669 BEQ Credit cSAaS ,Cloud BriONiX Live E69000OEI OR Gate 1200 USD Forward Think Blue ,Channel G660 @1.9 GHzEuroZone Stabilization ,Over Open Source IT Sector YDG 6 SG 3.0 Servers

Total Mobility Rank , No. 1 (Kape Sine Collaboration With CÆrrot Bay ?XCI 6.99724 Trillion $ to KR°°\••\Δ3.009.0.900 Y

The aftermath of decline in eBlue , Kape Sine is distributing R1 and E6 on NaNo Radio © and NaNo 100.

At Kapple Kape the new chip build would help translate and transfer data packets to free air.

Spectrum Charge is Omni.

Service Request would assume new signal path from 10 August 2021

#blockchain #cryptocurrency #crypto #data #help #help

World's No 1 Working NaNo Network. CBL 42000p at 6 Ghz. Visual IP bb.nn.k.ee.s.Cloud300[¶]Δ34 Billion $Δ\$\€\¥\$\\\•10 Year Yield.

The Recovery Kit includes new registration and regime as per internet standards.

6.99724 Trillion $ to KR°°\••\Δ3.009.0.900 Y

Yes Bank, Services GTRD to GPRS 1Df$

Executive Exchange over the Engine is 4.9878%

Total Mobility Rank , No. 1

World's First Hyper Media HyB 6000 Read Enabled eExchange. #bank #fintech #media #payments #news #payments #bitcoin #btc

Citibank US Bloomberg Businessweek Bloomberg Asia

HDFC Bank Canara HSBC Oriental Bank of Commerce Life Insurance Company Limited

HSBC

> *Neo-Globalization And the Computing Tools...They get expensive by the Day, CEO Channel Collaboration between Carrot Bay & BlueFedFin.*

Paper Blue 2.0 FFXC (R) TECHNOLOGY Survey

Project GOLDFISH SIX (6) is now loaded with external audit/accounting power.

The Graphic Code is reasonable and assumed to run without hurdles.

On the CHIP board I have tested a large amount of Experimental Data HEDGE and C-Type Capital Bonds.

C.E.W Quarter Analytics on Demand via DEMAT 5.6.2 DC Open.

The much needed cross section help from BlueFedFin is the invoice Inclusion to support Intelligence needs and BI Tools Appreciation.

It's a playground of Murphy's Apple and I am about to win that Jungle Safari!!

Here the market that we Understand from Kåpē INT FIN ,Kape Sine Cloud 690000.9880 INR

19779980.098 INR

GRAFIX GRAPH NODE::99867:8890

First Transaction Transmission , June 1,2021.

Company Charter & Annual Reports are delayed by 6 Months.

Share Quant CX44400:: # 5.8897%

Quantum Earnings:: Q1: 700 Million $

Q2: 6989 Million $

....A lot depends on Vector And Side Scaling methods.

A positive jump in the Market.

Kapple Kape 100000.978 HBMN11100000100.989

€° •••• 3.689 T $

$ •••••° 9.889 T $

£°•••°•• 111.988 T $

The Last Code Match is superior to the Exit Node.

*Company Net Usage For BEN is *5TER*

1000 Billion XSDaT SHARES

Total Market Swapping:: 70 Trillion $

Sweep In with YB, # 98.78%

BI Market With AI IP Net at BEN NaNo 6.^{0}

P^{n} :: 100∅ Trillion €

C^{n}:: 7000^{0n} Billion USD ($)

S 300.0898 A 109900090.988

iAC9.0 ? PaperBlue © 2030

Chairman Notes.

—–IEQS Office. 2021.2022.2023 Open

CHAPTER FIVE

MICRO ASIA 0-1 Why A Blog Matters?

I studied journalism in 2019-20 and found no real connect to the augmented field while conceiving content and the grammatical secret association. Many creative UI-UX agencies are stuck with passionately inclined new & fresh ideas to execute for example a TVC can bring to life a common notion and a song can change the mood of the apprentice. Gaming in the industry for nearly decades I havent come accros the service of the blue word in a case so out of place that we don't know how to act.

Blog is a baseband friend in partnership with set rules of operation under my belt.

Let me introduce you to the audacity work...

Let's DISCOVER #ZyNa © Blue Wave Technology

Lorose

The Login to Profound Artistry...only the Silicon Valley knows... Evidence of Experience!!

#BlueFedFinIxc #InternetAS50 #USRE 0.9895 INR 667.9890657

At the most advanced stages...we can state 3D #Fundamental and #Algorithmic Construction...

#Company holds important and one of the most expensive papers in IT & Science.

#Media Elementary Care is on for base station.

I would like to see a fresh garland and then enter the password to it.

Human Efforts will cautiously presume the horse power and hence be the voted winner. #smartcities #power #artificialintelligence

Branding A cloud takes away lot of heat....CBL is fast rotating the 50 Billion $ Mark post Reserve Reset. #construction #branding

We acknowledge that GoldFish SIX (6) will encounter mention on poverty but it's the least regarded place if poverty became a non secular issue. #technology #research #cloud #media

CÆrrot Bay will extend Electronic Clearance Services for BFF with Vase 1.0 on 24MP PaperBlue Signals.

-Karanvir Singh

FOUNDER CEO & CHAIRMAN

> *Serendipity √:: Common Data Classification Management , This is where the IntelliO Goes Zoom...Market Analysis ,Red Cloud 1.0 Fixed Bugs , >>OXb Account 670 Billion $>>*

Lorose

S1 Frame Takes 8 Bit DB Read Code

S2 Frame Takes 60 Bit DB ReD Cloud 1.0

S3 Frame Takes 92 Bit DVC Device CÆrrot 4.0

I am very much impressed with Technology that the theory about Serendipity has taken an insert.

I think one of the main Data Targets are Cohesive and Conducive of Cognitive Online Behaviour.

FA Service Blüē Would deal one on one with Emergence and Equality Features going beyond Advertisement and

Channel AI Read-Write Commands.

Citi Solutions Team is at 900 M $.

Industry Outlook is around 24 Billion $°•°{÷}

C1-1-100 Waiver (Citigroup)

Text 2 Data (T2D) , Text 2 Cloud (T2C) :The Open Architecture Choice: Going Digital For EXAT 100P. Project MintReX 1100 with AQS at 55 Billion $>>>

Lorose
Down Cast 24 Hours at 2$ From VaaS 3.0 to Class 5800, Ethernet Services.

The two Exchange the #Computing Assembly and Reform the Asset Council. Within the frame of a CXO , I see it's a double digit Investment in the fragmented media world... #Technology is Changing the #Socio-economic #Behaviour and there is not but one single choice to become inevitable by making a dominion of Public Events.

Project GOLDFISH SIX (6) - POWT Major Survey

CÆrrot #EDGE as #Virtual Stream and Flow Combines Data based Cloud Migration and Synaptic Touch to your Phone Screen.

#innovation

The Tx Main Set will focus on emissions via eFed and eNucleon 1000 , eFed has a 1 Bit Score and eNucleon will try and gather 24 Bit PaperBlue Stream. #technology

he Log pressures are an organic #Organisational input feed and the feedback loop needs to sort the actual variable strength of the Transmitter Signal. (BIO Network)© #investment #data #technology

By 2024 a few of the #cognitive properties and Product trends would push the AI Port to enable AaaS (Activation as a Service) #bigdata #ai

The number of #e-Transfers ☁?are going to be around 97% with Transactions & Data Transmission variances.

#Cloud OTS or One Time Services #Protocol © will enclose the IT Bandwidth and the Markets as Defacto Rational Endorsement.

As the #analytics Contract details become available we would be rolling the action plan for Large >>> 1970032413.9976

#ml (KREEP)- 6/^{9}00/^{00}∅9000^{n} ©

Spot Survey by Team FinBluê:99796-88-670+

Keynote to the European Markets;::;

Virtual Office makes notice of 50 Billion $>

S Market inflow to be dominant and serial ...cross investment will be Key.

The Radio Insertion –Under Reviews

While a Full Wave confirmation is awaited I m excited and engineered to gear OUT the shift BoX...Cloud is on Heavy Brent Rule...

Market would sit on a Mandate before PoWT. #like #opensource #bigdata #startups #ai #startup

Post InSipiaN 247 I would like to introduce NeoCoNEX 4.0.0 CBL Hyper Threading Link to Buffer the Data Packets. ?#technology

eBlue Investment Graph via Radio (50Billion $). #investing #data #cloud

CORE TRADING REST WITH KAPPLE 1Q13. #analytics #cryptocurrency

BlueFedFin Ixc is in a position to repool it's open source Technology Drift and Learnings from Quantum Data & AI & underline... #blockchain

Some Capital Gains are only averages and the real time fund datums are unique and Bio Net Compatible. #investment #finance #fintech

CÆrrot IntelliO will pick up MetaCalls and NaNo Radio Interior ETX Calling through out the Network.

111.87996 G RAQ 991887.97897 €€€ @ 78.996%

W2300 €€€€×××€€•••°••|•••°°=×××Δ$^¥|$•|

© Symbol One FëD.

Major Players:: Delta 1119 Transactions. Open Source €\$\¥\¢/£+ Yes Bank| Citigroup |HDFC | Fi

Crypto Asset Mapping Is coming around in July 21, we will accelerate into fast flow Economy 11E .-CEO

US Market inflow to be dominant and serial ...cross investment will be Key.Product Cost is an internal priority and to bring the revenue Figures I am supplicating with SPeCTrON 1000 ,Audit Intelligence and Analytics .

Enter Caption

#TeamFinBlue #CEO #CXO Citibank Europe

Karanvir Singh

Founder CEO & Chairman

carrotbaysxci.ceo@protonmail.com

800 M $ -HTAP Credit to Bank Market : IXC Model – OLAP Confirmity & Transmission Dial UP @ 128 Billion USD-CAD IPQ Rewards

Lorose

Powerhouse Economy and a subtle system of Financial Export, Carrot InteLLIO will draft 800 M $ in access condition to BIG Data and AI -FIN Format Bonds.

Why CRYPTO is Under Sold ?? Can eBlue win CRYPTO 1.0 ?

Online Bank Process will assume DFQ Figure 100 and Scale to Online Resources and Side-Segment JOB making.

With production assets of 480.0979 Billion $. Its a multi format guard at bay to proceed with FINTECH and CBDC

Programmes.

HTAP Engima......

Hybrid transaction/analytical processing (HTAP), a term created by Gartner Inc. – an information technology research and advisory company. As defined by Gartner:

Hybrid transaction/analytical processing (HTAP) is an emerging application architecture that "breaks the wall" between transaction processing and analytics. It enables more informed and "in business real time" decision making.

Source : Wikipedia

With OLAP its a medow in the cloud and the market look essentially bare and full framed by incursion.

OLAP with Full Stack Nano Radio would discover Graphics Pipeline. More e Blue and More TX Power Hours.

> *CAÆROT Bay SXCi, HTAP TeLCOS 1.0 , Listening Globe and Chairman Features. CAÆROT Bay SXCi | 4000K : Cloud BIG Business 2000 CXO Rights...BI BIA and CEO Shuffle. (800.999£)*

Lorose

CAÆROT Bay SXCi

At the beginning of the year we had one idea one execution strategy...this lead into inventory innovation and we adopted mentions from calls.

This summer it's the safe practices.

At 498% the total mobility charge on CAÆROT IntelliO 700 is 643.868 Billion $.

32798.079

112.99865 Trillion /$ Data Stakes and ViX E213 Stock is 590.2212 Billion /USD.

Strong Outputs are expected towards the next decade and there would be EXAT 1A of 669%>

New parameters around Analytics and HTAP..will fetch 430% of New Data Entries.

Q1 : 6647.978

Q2 : 44697.99

Q3 : 776988.68907

Q4 : 8897199089.978

EQWS4678000IN400SDF5767D107

The mode of behaviour will express the Graphic Set and Integration Soft Launch is something we are working on.

I hope this makes the Market move towards more informed decisions.

6D Routing Wire XFC A449780000Y64B

eblue.service247@gmail.com

eBlue Commitment # .gov .Pvt .Inc

6000 Billion Page Missions..Direct D Funnel.

HR Program: DFC5478000 DWT Week 1 – 3.

Investment Portfolio:: 664612W758090S

CÆrrot this: FF55512235EDS658 CODE XC 11

Global Cyber Adoption for a Single Payline Wire and eBluÊ 400S are successfully appreciated and appraised. 7 Trillion $ Coast Query...Can Amazon Diverge Energy... Earnings!!

BlueFedFin Ixc , The Fetching Hot Wire Stuff and the Global Cyber Adoption for a Single Payline Wire and eBluÊ 400S are successfully appreciated and appraised.

The new excitement is the #blockchain theory and ledger Cost...The KPI's at Zero EXAT are Performing Well by Radio Graded.Nano Radio will ferry the Graph XCE Radio for successful Execution.

As CEO I m enthralled about the enthusiasm for Fintech in and around...the ecosystem is basically drawn from #innovation #startups #smartcities #cyber .

A lot of research would be Sorted and before the Settlement Wire confirms the Code and Project I am assured that we would be breaking the Monetary SPE Q1 – Q4.

Cloud SPECTRON HAS 512GB and is ready to launch the multi channel Deals.

Production Goals as SaaS ,IaaS and VaaS tools will work into aggressive coalition and IOT Vendetta Planning.

#cybersecurity #crypto #research #cloud #work #ceo #project #iot #infrastructure #fintech #hybridcloud

#azure #amazon

CÆrrot Bay SXCi will remain AI Virtual TeLCOS Partner and Bluetooth Range Contributors.

WH Deal at 6.8879 Trillion $>>

#CEO

#cloudcomputing $$$$

> *ENERGY COMMISSION, Commitment Channel Charges 40 Billion USD. eBlue TX 45 at Bay with International IntelliO and PaperBlue ISx Global NaNo RADIO Full Frame Discovery.*

Lorose

Net Focus on Networking System Expansion is on Upscale Coordinates. Business Reference is Debt OUT Plugin.The last Decade seems a happy Spot on a 100 Million User Base for FINTECH CONTENT and Contextual Habit and Behaviour.?

The real plan is to outnumber the fancy Dr Advice...Generate Green Income Derivatives and a Splash HEDGE .

Global Market:: 4798.9980

After the restrictions lift up we are seeking close collaboration with Media Techs and Neo Finance for a Strategic Panel Fit in IOT AND CLOUD.☁?☁?

300% Mobility On Backend and Frontdesk Reviews.

Lending License and Creative Common HYPE

PaperBlue would seek a full spectrum use and processing at 50Gbps. Neural Networks will assume Artificial STATiC Station Inbox.

*3D Analysis and Market GRAPHiX Meta Data Sharing on BFF Site with Project SPeCTrON *���*

@<< 56 Million $>> (Information Technology) Payrolls Including.

Making Contractual Experience and BE Hotspot around the Globe.

GPCN First On Planet, The E /CARRY Flux Currency that KREEP WOULD EXCHANGE. Evidence DEBIT 100 Trillion KR by 2050. Oxxy Blue Gets Launch For GIO PAPERBLUE AND GIO INTERNET INTELLIO.

Lorose

You gotta get the Market to release the Channel of OSF Marketing and then get Money Research knowing the EXAT.Corporate Communications can be now passed on PsyGram 5.0. I am absolutely convinced with the story board and would like to personally reformat the DM Switch. ECB TQ 100 is an instrument based SIM Query PARC Packet Convertible D Type Cloud CCY Compliance. I m investing a crop of Banking Ethics and Government Fellowship.

The Host Terminal creates the ownership Program and CB Live © Goes 24/7.

Neural Networks and IPD Financial Intelligence Services pool is 23.568 Trillion $>>>

I am seeking a payment line from our Banking Officio Partners.

Linkage and CyberSecurity is Looping between the EXTerIoN and SPeCTrON Units.

AAQ 1000

I m hopefull, the next 6 Months will see 700% AI CYCINOR and AI Stock XVC Internet with IntelliO working at 500%.

PaperBlue EChip Program is Accessible And Transmission will be recorded.

Our residency change plans are viewing normal credit.

Taking forward the Blue Services Badge.

#PoWT #KaranvirSingh

LDS :Q1,Q2,Q3,Q4 NANO RADIO IOT 11.00.1318

CHAPTER SIX

India 2 Micro Asia - A FIN Assessment & Investment Technology

SERENDIPITY, Service Blüē, Set Matrix 2.9.0, SPeCTrON 2.0 2030, Studio Carrot Bay, TEAM INTELLIO 5490 PATCH, TRAINING CLOUD GOO, Virtual Chip Set, WALLSTREET, XCS Cloud Intuitive Services, XDR Cloud 1.9.1313, XoN Cloud 5.43.89X

The above given cloud tags are responsible for mobile and IOT Insertions and Case Value doubles when these emissions make the OS Glow and Speak.

India 5.0 + 15.9978 Trillion $ by 2025:

Lets fix the agenda:

Everything Virtual doesn't fit the bill...but at CÆrrot "Everyone" VIRTUAL is the Moto.

Let's begin at IntelliO with integrated & agile soft approach to Trade, Banking ,Jobs , Finance , Global Advertising & Interior Marketing.

> *"It seems probable that once the machine thinking method had started, it would not take long to outstrip our feeble powers... They would be able to converse with each other to sharpen their wits. At some stage, therefore, we should have to expect the machines to take control."-Alan Turing*

Lorose

At the end of Supply Chain Operations to here's what growth means; An Expedition par Excellence.

Office of Internal Governance makes us Broadcast the Unique Data Environment and BI-AI Grid just complements the Tornado.*

If you are inclusive with high intensity intellectual discovery come join us for a brainstorming session.

All over a cup of coffee and donuts!! ?

**(Market Based Investment and Infrastructure Stock & Identical Instruments.)*

> *India is amongst the fastest growing tech economies and it has Transformation Ready*

Networks. Ready IOT + Cloud AI at a 700 Billion $ Price. DPA And more....

Lorose

An early start to #Summer was Never on our cards..I could have installed the DPA (Digital Protocol Alliance) #Contract with #Certificate, but we delayed the calculus. Now it's the Frozen #Call and we are Ready.☁?

This harmony between man & machine is so vibrant, it just removed the shackles.

Somewhere down the ladder the process is still an anonymous drag of #InvertedBLOCKCHAIN, but it is forming the #Calculated Results.

Global Newsrooms Are Now Super-Chromatic... Thanks to Serendipity!!

The industry would and could expect the fair side of this New #Technology and use it as per potency.

#digital #manufacturing #innovation #marketing

India is amongst the fastest growing tech economies and it has Transformation Ready Networks.

Cyber Security is the much needed acquisition along with Electronic Money.

#fintech #cybersecurity #ai #iot #data

As #Data #Substance is Realized we can move ahead and win our proxy settings. #cloud #india

It's a #BIG Logical factor that the two types of Intelligence simultaneously interacts with the Network and is developing into a Lotus.

SYSTEM IMPROVEMENT AND MORE PHONIC & STABLE SIGNALS WILL BRING CLARITY TO THE SPECTRA.✈?

#artificialintelligence #money #network

#WebAddressCXO1 #PW

#DPA is Implemented!!

Federal Bank HSBC Global Banking and Markets

Business Standard #marketsegmentation

900 Billion $

IOT-Cloud SPeCTrON comes from NaNo

Categories of Digital Formalization and Algorithm Specific Radio Utilities

–Business Report

CÆRROT INTELLIO SSRT 2 TESTING 1QE400 E BLÜĒ 100 MILLION

Cloud SPeCTrON comes from NaNo Categories of Digital Formalization and Algorithm Specific Radio Utilities.

At present it cost around 300 Billion $ to receive the SPeCTrON 1.2.36 Cloud Hangout To Price The Shell..

Everything seems well received within the framework and I m only Citing the crucial meta data.

Pulling this to the market..I think it's a very bright choice to emancipate via TrueBlue. So all in all PaperBlue will take up additional resources and Internet Chaos while retrieving the source and the cell.

For now we have a Brent table looking at 5.9887 Trillion $ by 2030.

That we will see around.

CÆrrot this: 441768E5700

CÆRROT INTELLIO SSRT 2 TESTING 1QE400 E BLÜĒ 100 MILLION

Lorose

Cloud SPeCTrON comes from NaNo Categories of Digital Formalization and Algorithm Specific Radio Utilities.

At present it cost around 300 Billion $ to receive the SPeCTrON 1.2.36 Cloud Hangout To Price The Shell..

Everything seems well received within the framework and I m only Citing the crucial meta data.

Pulling this to the market.I think it's a very bright choice to emancipate via TrueBlue. So all in all PaperBlue will take up additional resources and Internet Chaos while retrieving the source and the cell.

For now we have a Brent table looking at 5.9887 Trillion $ by 2030.

That we will see around.

CÆrrot this:

Global Cyber Adoption for a Single Payline Wire and eBluÊ 400S are successfully appreciated and appraised. 7 Trillion $ Coast Query...Can Amazon Diverge Energy... Earnings!!

Lorose

BlueFedFin Ixc , The Fetching Hot Wire Stuff and the Global Cyber Adoption for a Single Payline Wire and eBluÊ 400S are successfully appreciated and appraised.

The new excitement is the #blockchain theory and ledger Cost...The KPI's at Zero EXAT are Performing Well by Radio Graded.Nano Radio will ferry the Graph XCE Radio for successful Execution.

As CEO I m enthralled about the enthusiasm for Fintech in and around...the ecosystem is basically drawn from #innovation #startups #smartcities #cyber .

A lot of research would be Sorted and before the Settlement Wire confirms the Code and Project I am assured that we would be breaking the Monetary SPE Q1 – Q4.

Cloud SPECTRON HAS 512GB and is ready to launch the multi channel Deals.

Production Goals as SaaS ,IaaS and VaaS tools will work into aggressive coalition and IOT Vendetta Planning.

#cybersecurity #crypto #research #cloud #work #ceo #project #iot #infrastructure #fintech #hybridcloud #azure #amazon

CÆrrot Bay SXCi will remain AI Virtual TeLCOS Partner and Bluetooth Range Contributors.

WH Deal at 6.8879 Trillion $>>

#CEO

#cloudcomputing

CÆrrot this:

What's an Artificial Brand Puzzle?? IntelliO Fires Defaults!!!

What's an Artificial Brand Puzzle??

A Market with 2$ Price Tag...!!

Project GOLDFISH SiX (6) takes measures in a few nautical miles...where does marketing branding go in the making of a sustainable product...??☁?

Poverty lines are throwing a gateway of hope out of Liquid Measures and Organic Instances are available at threshold of Maximum Fund Gains and Truly adopting a Free Economy.

A great introspection into how the world would see it...

19989.978

4553289.9980

600 Billion $ on Commission Ideas... Rate Percent of 98.757 %

EXAT Quality 9.9 Q1 598.878B $ [€]×××•

eBlue Reserve Currency Cyc PsyGram 7.0

> *Project NILE X1 , INTERNATIONAL MARKET PARADIGM. Our Full Frame Review. D2C Competent , CÆRROT FLIGHT TO Red Sea!! (90.00£)*

Lorose
EV 500, The World Mix That Flashed Our Boardrooms.

What otherwise could have been a Cross Word Call.. turns out to be a Paradox, A Chaos Theory ,A Set of Unified Matrix and the 40 Billion Euro € Drive Around Colaba (South Bombay).

I personally Reload this to Memory as the Road to Perdition and Passionate Inventions. By the Days, By the Grace of Computing.

One Real Outcome of the Experiment at BFF did get me in the Track Socket but the Ports work fine.

A Top Priority under my belt is the revival of New Equilibrium and A Not So High Price of Honest Presumptions.

Blue End Network is dedicated to Superficial/Artificial Support. BEN is a 70 Billion$ Express Experiential Line through Business Parks and had been at the Meeting Practon For me.

BEN 2 CÆRROT :(990)

ADASx Shares 1000 Million

TiPCoin 556.989

ForTCoin 447989.99

Stage 2 Carrier Frequencies CBAY 600Mhz -RAM Fix 1.3.41313

Welcome to the Virtual Desk ...We are designing the best found in Cloud Finance...Take A Seat To Take a Hot Cup of Codes!!

SID 66:55:34:900 GSQ
Stage 2 Carrier Frequencies

Δ ××¢|CFx 5.0

€=6.00909 | $=9.09987

#CEOPort6
#CitiMarkUp #CodeBody
#CoreGeneration #Intel
Or Should We See #Vegas

+60.89$ :: Serial Sequence Slot Load of 51 Billion $:c: #CÆrrot

1000.899+

GG SG 7.0 Internet Lake Studio 440Q 13.23 S

Call it Neo Risk !! This one out to #Citi Citibank US Citibank Hall

Radio Interferometry:: When we first thought about

Radio Sky the distribution of inferences was not just gaining interstellar powers to achieve the randomness in the job. I could only spend a night on it and what was observed was a fine discovery. I laughed and made a precursor to objectify the Trivia that came to my mind. Digital Sky would bring the first 100 Million into AI Stock: This is Credited as Project Nile X1 :: Only to get this done Independently we chose Events that Projected our Probability Policy. We have been running around Banks This could be called a valid closure to the Settlement. Thank You for Bridging the GAP+

#CEO

#Fed10D

#India
Bloomberg+ (9007Y 0/9FQ|~Δ)

> *CÆrrot Bucket Guest at G7, PoWT Full Volume Discovery, Invention, Investment and Interior.700 Trillion $*

Lorose

CÆrrot Paper Corporate (, HT) , (C) , (BFF)

I take this opportunity to conclude one of the best offerings on table i.e Project GOLDFISH SIX(6).

At CÆrrot IntelliO we publicly went 700 Billion $> Initiative At Cost Coast in Cash.

What it delivers is a huge connect to 40 Trillion $ Debt...

International IntelliO produced Sun Scotch...☁?

Otherwise, the ruling body makes Goldfish SiX interesting in the coming years.

As long as we decide to park at Cyber 1 & 2 ...it would be a huge amount of good insight, intuitive knowledge and scientific practice to resolve poverty once and for all..

CBDC control room has triggered us eBlue in the known frame.

Global Guest Seeking is around 500 Million.

User # 5880

Citigroup- Citibank US KS -7000

CHAPTER SEVEN

Micro ASIA - The Root Cure To Practical Economy.

SXCi ; The Factor that Ruled the New World Order...A New Age Call that could have gone missing.Here it is ...the first repulsive action from -CÆRROT BAY SXCÏ.

Lorose

SXCi was never a huge bid as much as the condition Demand in Neo Finance, I took forward the Initiative to make International Banking Industry come out of the W7 Debts. That is a top priority right now because this way we can proceed with the idea of Discrete Progress.

Ask for the program and You will realize the dream is bigger than just being a part of Traditional Success. It's a Free Code Asset And Assembly for A TU 4 Scale and would see a Family of experience around eC/B° Blue.

#bankingindustry #finance #experience #economy #entrepreneurship #startups

Acting on the legal philosophy I can gauge the guarantee and along with it the walk to #Freedom.

Digital Store ,Street Database and Bluetooth Wireless Payment Intelligence System, LCxO 1360/DC is going to walk away the waiting period from 2013-2020/+- 9(#F eFox CC #Hedge Fund Gainers) ↖?

Bio Network Implementation and HBC Guidance is a top priority Too.

At the Group it's a practical dream and a Quote for a Quote scenario.

#LSE – FDxCV 44.168/0010HA #CITIBANK London #database #network #blockchain

AI Feedback D4 6 (MP U) Service #MdaaS

#BloombergRadio

#CarrotBay

SiSBlue 2000 Upgrade::: The #BEXTRON DBMS goes live....6 B € /$ @ Δ 9.9967 and EXAT CC V 1 RELVAR 20 @ 996%

Lorose
The NEXT Board Round will help us decline unwanted wait and close the Recovery Futures.

#finance #ai #fintech

I consider this an evolutionary move to Bring OTSC (©),AI Contextual & Database Exchange and Information in line with the Production. #deeplearning

NEW YORK QW WHQ PB 11Q11000 LOCAL & INTERNATIONAL OxxyBlue 3.0

A huge semantics Intervention is proposed in the incentive Phase and Stage 1 – 6 in the next 5 Years. #dataanalytics #datascience

This comes along with Tx(Transmission) eBluÊ & eFed with EXTerIoN Cloud 100 Extension Computer Grading. #machinelearning

Looking Forward to the #Genius of Geometry...& Calculus. #bigdata #artificialintelligence

Offline Cloud Interception Quality Targets 99.997#TeX 7000 #quality #help #database #cloud

CÆrrot Bay ?XCI

CÆrrot this:

Why GoldFish SIX will challenge every financial entity and beat the roots of the entire world's Commercial Activities and Business Administration. Why we are the company Next Door. (8£)/99654-66-5431

Lorose

The very future held back by #business models and the Financial draft held under government , public, private and independent is so surreal that our imagination has a new neighbour.

New Age #Technology was the key in the last decade , we never saw the digital spinning, we never caught wind for AI.

Today the everything and everyday solutions are by far the modern new choices of the #Nations striving strictly for a positive , productive and personal use.

It's time the developed world meets the counterpart and competitive #Nudge from developing Countries.

Poverty is curable, poverty is inside the grasp of logic and hence be sorted by our automated diplomacy.

A humble appeal to the Central Banks and Global Corporations to assist through the journey.

A final bell and the last version of the fight ; Feed All , Respect All.

Chief Economist ,

GoldFish SIX /009007/907675-1887

-Economic Agenda & Manifesto Talks for #GoldFish SIX (6)

Citibank US

CHAPTER EIGHT

Micro (e) & Asia Together

Who is Micro "é" Enabled?

My task is to finish the length of one object and one subject....

The following blog entries are GSM Mapped to relay the command:

Fintech FIST (First Instructions System Terminal) 6.9954 Trillion $[€]\$$\¥¥¥ Δ 0.0019346CCS KREEP Exchange Works International. 20 Billion € EXAT On One Blüē CXUI WAP 200 LineLIVE © PAPERBLUE®[2021-2026]

Lorose

SEATTLE VFXC 1000 @

Paper Blue WQX 1000::[™] [©]::: #CEO

[Citi Private Bank] √Δ4.99890/ 199987754392.9678 INR+/009011#(4£)

#economy

To incubate the memory location and Process Net (Non) Zero #Transition in a phased manner the #CÆrrot IntelliO would induct the principal Transmission Channel Collaborating with BFF Federal (9C) Fund #Execution #Program and the #CFO Instructions. #cloudcomputing

A register address would presumably creat the eBlue 1000 and OxxyMedia 1 Blüē on Tag Cloud and xET 1.0 Computing.

#cybersecurity #data #hardware

xET 1.0 DAC #BINARY is now available for VC 1 and VC 2. This would be a sequence and outline policy for INTERNET and Routed Hardware.√

#computing

A 4 Trillion $\€\¥

|<•••°°°•••> | *0.0089+/Δ*

19.9968 €.

10 Billion StakeFIN to Savings Bank Computing ATX Engine for the first FIN 1 (Fintech FIST) Licenced Tx (AAS4000) [Root 11.]√

First Hitting #Currency #Hybrid Meta-Trade Graphic and FIN Execution B11 and B13 are connected on DAC BINARY and Crypto Wire Number. +(99979979.99780/ 9000-92&9912# #trading #currency #blockchain #trading #currency #cryptocurrency

CÆrrot EDGE is on TelcoMatic Automation Mode and the Neural Feedback SDX 10.0 could copy Wave GA 1V4.0 for the #Storage Blüē 1EQ.

#CEO #CFO #CMO

Bloomberg New Economy Forum

CÆrrot this:

Project SPeCTrON: Post Inhibition Economy and World Poverty Guidelines...#WeAreNotSlaves. A True American Optimisation and the Chief Resources of the World...Why we need to rescue our planet...??

Lorose

Project SPeCTrON will in time be processing and navigating the present and the future poverty Combination of several economies and industry standards via the Blue Prism Network.

It's an exciting time in the Future and that we will gift our generations a slavery free Economic System and End Point of Monetary -Judiciary Formats and endurance of insurance against financial frauds.

Many a times we pledge our work towards Excellence and that explains a vivid notion that we need a surplus world and workforce that cuts pre-economuc condition of the State of Finance in the New World.

I am strikingly pointing at Digital Migration and Cloud and AI as our true meaningful friends in collaborating with a Larger Universe.

For poverty it's clear that our Governments must meet our prejudice and pre-conditioned impact of putting every pocket at Test..

I believe our reciprocating nature will benefit from equality... inclusion and the test if time in order to serve this protocol.

Human Rights are a Challenge that needs moral prime spot handling and great convergence in between Media and the Government.

We must conclude that it's the greatest of nations to decide first on its economy and defences by surrogating the new Alliances.?

As PoWT makes risen statements ...Its my honoured duty and promise to settle every Transaction with Reality.

Team FinBluê for PoWT

CÆrrot will adopt PaperBlue Technology and Sophisticated Hardware-Software Experience.#CEO XS-AE + 600.978 Billion € [°°°••|•°°] (NaNo Radio Plug) LQT 1000 SHARES going in the Vaults.

Lorose

PaperBlue is just a Digital Switch between TX and TCx Lines , we love the spectrum processing and it's a positive Figure out of the box strategy.

PB 1.0.33.9 Goes Live with CBL Collaboration Interchange of<<< 100 Billion $>>>>>••°•|BlueFedFin Ixc.

At BlueFedFin a host of Client-Customer Channel with Beta CEO is running at full throttle.

No Station Differential would be suggested to the Cloud Environment with Market Strategy being Built Back Stack Delivery.

It's a complementary assembly and the router takes care of the Prints.

Feeling Runtime and Real-time Shows and IDVX Views.

Analytical Engine and the Compute Engine will step between the Core MARKET.

CÆrrot will adopt PaperBlue Technology and Sophisticated Hardware-Software Experience.

#CEO

CÆrrot this: FF547578CT687

CHAPTER NINE

CEO BROADCAST DB 1000X- Micro ASIA

1Bit Processing, Analytics CBY, Analytics Chart, Audio Network, Banking, Battery, BEXTRON 1, BEXTRON 1900, BIC System, Billion Students, BLUE SERVICES 24HRS, Blue Ten Bond, BOSTON, C100PENFIN, CANADA VIA USA ..UK CANADA 667, CARROT EXTERION, CBL CÆrrot 1@100, CEO, CFO, Chicago, Chip Clouds UE440000

CEO | 5G COMMONS & CLOUD

CÆrrot Communication MaaS Stage II & Monetisation

CBAY - Base 3.0 Ghz

I am really excited as the CEO to know new targets and bounce back to normalcy. Channel Cast 1.0 CEO PacKETS worth 60 B $

Lorose

With too much freedom discipline makes the way for excellence.

BlueFedFin Ixc proves an excellent feature to Credit Creation and Repo Building.

I am really excited as the CEO to know new targets and bounce back to normalcy.

This is the executive chamber where the technology rates the council money.

#money #ceo #technology #building #gains

Project SPeCTrON 1.0 , A CÆRROT INTELLIO INITIATIVE. (US)

Lorose

Project SPeCTrON 1.0 Client-Server Delivery Set.

With workforce tightening I am able to analyse the Market Introduction post Covid as a great recession.

In the room I have a secure post as the powerful Technology Dictates.

Keeping on the positive thumb positions I have a see through approach while the Automatic Simulation proceeds with a close 500 Billion $>.

The numbers I have from Radio Cast 4.0 are crucial in defying the odds in the Job.

SPeCTrON 1.0 will source Production queries and make H+ Intelligence grow and provide us the necessary insights around global infrastructure planning.

Flash OEM Rates 56.899% to 1500.887%

Generation: 6.YEQ//90006//001001#

BloombergAsia

Trade VEX Vector Support to SPeCTrON 2.0 will start with a collaborative session with BlueFedFin Ixc. from July 2021.

Coming Up Next NES Shares @carrotcloudai .

1000.0980 Million ¥°°•°××°••√500.00

198% Market Throw Up Rate for Bond EMQ Front at the CLOUD SPeCTrON 4000 SG 1.1.2.4 (IPNet)

-CEO,CFO, CTO!

CÆrrot this:

What is SPeCTrON 1.0 Going to do to the international markets...A Global+ and a Rebound State. +US Debt Resolve!! Watch it Live ,Cloud EXTerIoN 1.6S

Lorose

Cast Bay Resolution Meter 40D , 40.990 Trillion $ Masking Ratio between the Next 20 Years.

CHAPTER TEN

Micro DEFENCE - AN INFRA PLAYOUT BUILD

The development system is logically derived from Cloud - AI & BI the very first step is the analog between new and old. I believe as CEO it was important to give time to the paradox and symmetrically observe the patterns of Trade & Business here.*

Micro Defence 3.3.3 is sophisticated and over powered. The pledge here is so strong that it wont retort any Business Sentiment. I have for you the ultimate holy grail of cosmic exuberance to BIX 9000. A promised stock of liquidity beyond perpetual grounds and rather a used touch of magical medicine.

Climate Change & Active Calls on Carbon Emissions

Lets follow the blog to Carrot MaaS (Media as a Service)...

The Next Live CB would capture data cards and solid state Architecture. 69 Trillion $ Sweep IN. [600.0£]

Cloud Blue Live- Beta OTSC 2013 Onwards

Tx Line (99879.9989)+700000/90+PaperBlue ©

EXAT Target is 698.9978 GQ (800)

For AI Choice Pattern Change within the International Market will plug new features and context to investment.

#money #ai #data

Data Wire eBlue 4000 ,Will look for minimum mining Currency Output.

Product Value for CBL is 40 M $.

#KeyNote11350 #Official

Tx Line (99879.9989)+700000/90+PaperBlue ©

EXAT Target is 698.9978 GQ (800)☁?

For AI Choice Pattern Change within the International Market will plug new features and context to investment.

#money #ai #data

Data Wire eBlue 4000 ,Will look for minimum mining Currency Output.??

Product Value for CBL is 40 M $.?

#KeyNote11350 #Official

Yellow Card, 20 Billion $ HXT-Wire From FIN ONE TECHNOLOGY SYSTEM, BLOCKCHAIN TX TESTING, CYBER NANO EXC 1 @ 2$ EXAT EC 1000 , Exchange

Lorose
39989.0009 V F 11195887.9890 BBD

The busiest route to FIN AI #Telegraph is Cloud Blue Live.

In 2015 when the universe around was a vivid #Complexity I reviewed the Corner Seat and took an exit exuberance for a moral delight.

The Business came into being after a record assimilation and research efficacy.

A free state system is a unique Assembly for the New #Age Existence of a Debt Free Economy.

World's No 1 Cyber NaNo Radio ! (Polyphonic)

#research #economy

The #Governance Pattern today is world class , enigmatic and exceptional.

> ***World's First and #World No. 1 Cyber NaNo Radio was a brainchild that came to existence from the stock ready Intelligence produced by Cloud Blue Live © -Chairman***

Lorose

#ai #ceo #business

> ***"I am immensely Impressed by the excellence inside CBL & NaNo Radio...Next Move Collaboration and Blockchain Inclusion."-CEO (From Strategy Review)***

Lorose

CÆrrot this: KV553424719000DF678

On fundamentals ,we recognize this opportunity to work on some of the behavioural practices in the industry and there exposure.
Vision 2030,as part of the program is now under Supervision.

77 U-445.654.00 1.0 AB-E642124

iX Business WebStore

Lorose
Industrial Exposure On Online Behavior /Kapple Kape Exclusive

Day 1

My slackware has new Jobs.They are listed with us as off office hours today and can be accessed with the USER ID formulated as per behavioural practice.

Day 2

An investment Cycle for on-line readership can be redeemed around 2020.

A 700 Million Dollar support infrastructure is advocated and will be in place by 2025.
2 Trillion Dollars of conceptual revenue streams are put in place to curb economic conjecture.
75% of all payments records received at our end will be processed as credit overlaps for audit purpose.

Employee engagement can be seen as default measurement for income authentication schemes.
A rate of 56% Growth Method Targets is under review for the market in advance

How to Write?

Where to acknowledge?

Higher Gross

Lower Gross

Plan to Market

Market to Mode 1

CEO CFO/CIO Report to Report OPEL.

Share Market as DSEQ Term 12090

CCO

Author's Corner

In 2014 I decided to enroll myself for BEA 101 X on Edx.org. Hardly did i know that i was going to be exercising the BE principles.

Further indictment to our notices is pending with the Legal Department. I acknowledge the wonderful association with Blue Funds that a week.

$24.5 Trillion worth of blue transactions are under process. Affinity to new business undertakings is on the charts. New assessment for the current fiscal is subject to change in the future. Our market segment growth is higher than the usual norms i.e. Group A1G investments.

$60 Billion of shared expenditure has been sanctioned for adequate credit supply towards the maturity of level 1 Funds. (FundBlue™).

CARROT BAY SXCI has played a pivotal lead role in organizing for us the KB.

"*About Me*"

As long you stay in the Entrepreneurial Domain You are the Main Actor and the main Subsidy of the Business Undertakings. This time I have a magical wand and I am interested in blowing away phantom and force to the industry & the ministry.

Anti-phishing Laws and the truth behind the ceremonial walls. Better value supply and the Side Chain Method of Developing Scientific business ideas and calculating upon Integrity and Technological advancement in the New World.

I am an Amritsar Born strict lover of art and exubcrance and this happens to be my turning instance of the moment to surprise everyone with an Institution Par Excellence in Academic Literature.

The SPHINX is REAL.

Check out:

https://ikvsingh.wordpress.com/

https://carrotbaysxci.wordpress.com/

www.ingramcontent.com/pod-product-compliance
Ingram Content Group UK Ltd.
Pitfield, Milton Keynes, MK11 3LW, UK
UKHW062313290726
14090UKWH00018B/1048